5 0 *H E*
A D S T
O N Y T
R E H Y

APPLE PIE EDITIONS

ISBN: 978-09539367-5-5

Published
Apple Pie Editions, Manchester, UK
Editor Phil Davenport

Design www.axisgraphicdesign.co.uk,
Manchester, UK
Print Compass Press Ltd
Typeset in FS Lola by Fontsmith

Acknowledgements
Thanks to Phil Davenport, Sue Collins, Alan Johnston, Ulrich Rückriem & Tessa Howe, Alan Ward, Mark Jalland, Avril Heffernan, for their support and inspiration. Also Prof. Graham White for his situations, fluents and actions. and the artist, nameless, thanks for the title.

0. For Gerard and Millice: 1

Contents

1. Content
2. Calculus
3. CBT
4. City
5. Cleverness
6. Colours
7. Compromise
8. Dialect
9. Doubt
10. Entscheidungsproblem
11. Epigones
12. Eugenics
13. Expectation
14. Faces
15. Family
16. First
17. Fishing
18. Fluents
19. Hesitation
20. Houses
21. Interference
22. Islam
23. Lassitude
24. Lime
25. Lottery
26. Method
27. Moment
28. Neither
29. Number
30. Objects
31. Palindrome
32. Place
33. Poem
34. Pornography
35. Professionalism
36. Quiescence
37. Reassurance
38. Reciprocity
39. Sculpture
40. Shaman
41. Singularity
42. Tmesis
43. Translation
44. Underachievement
45. Vinculum
46. Whorosphere
47. Widerstand
48. Yggdrasill
49. Apology

Content

0. *Contents* stroke executive summary: men never swim until they can, motionless, our standard redundancy and choice mildnesses expound the distentions: a base category of poetic situations or rather situation descriptions: as antimony, the frame orthodox treatment: with Moments, Fluents (propositional pseudogenes), Apologies (labelled transitions between states). Iff there are a finite number of models, *any closeness order we like* comes by surjective choice of vocabulary – reading struggle for perspective adjacency. One of the two routes is open, then that route can be travelled; if the other route is open, then that route can be travelled: iff both are open, then the two possibilities miraculously cancel each other out: neither. N+1 is the discrete breather I'm allowed to ask and see under-arching vinculums through the past pain, the puncturings, the distressed vintages – content importance we assign to early texts, when to compromise generates only compromise, content, its properties left wanting lacks artifice and the properties of its vehicle, (a) zero hopeful solidifies absence through non-zero, standing despite all plausibilities to fall, to a rational number equal to happening: 1

Calculus

0. monotonic the fall. In the cot, of equilibria and reducing complexities, the baby recognised my death as our eyes another reason to avoid the butchery of children's moment Cut, a form of transitivity when the engine stops and you can't go on, but you get out of the car and go on. A prepersonal intensity corresponding to the passage one experiential state of the body to another implying augmentation or diminution in that body's capacity to act She reminded me of what we could have had – and it was remarkably paradisiacal, only less so. The dynamics hovering bird wings, the public are mad those that aren't found in any species in city park ascriptions of method. Two opposing points connected by positive and negative charge tired but it was there, something about never getting there – the slender margin language object – daily routine of back and forth sine wave study to the quaint notions of windswept steppe and desert's unequal presumption of innocence without fear of retributive access will be the end of memory: 1

CBT

0. for it to be nice save your rapture and replace it; Therapy is not prostitution penetration is safe customer care from punishment as there's no permanent damage, dulled by repetition, ceasefires or resolutions: an enforced homosexual encounter until it is too late. I close my eyes. Predictively bad for musicality if you opened the door without saying unwritten rules: assumptions stroke expectations govern an employee's working relationship with the employer appropriate for subsequent use. Repulsed (draped in blue): your gaze, with semen dripping from my face, masturbate on my knees opening to say something for some time – I have destroyed something beautiful. Who I was with What was I doing When was it Where was I the mechanical calculated aspect of gestures rather than frenzied, offered no resistance, laboured to please, eager and committed no more virginally tentative, derogated effectiveness counters our consolation through interference patterns of net and skin. Without independent media, to compromise, to accept barbarous dissolution, embracing flowers, the worst thing that could happen is an absolute future that looked bleak for vertebrates: 1

City

0. Finally a poset to celebrate, stacked volumes alternating sequence of vertices and edges, a walk curatorially driven relaxed histocompatibility, the totality of living humans, insofar as one belongs to its tranquil fianchetto in time we have the solidity of buildings in space as it extended into projective geometry, a soldier died for perspective, pancyclic adjacent and degree. Ignore the gaps beyond meniscus edge the difference only snips as geography alphabet which shapes Abelian thoughts. Renormalisation avoids limitations of infinity; steel glass, music of voices reach out their Hill sphere, sanitary in a good way, sterile in a good way, childfree in a good way, implying a good way infinities that interchange this/that/them/there/not here. Joy of landing. Scaffolding, ephemeral, celebrating construction and noise. Reject nature in a good way. This fact, our mind seems to utilize this fact, makes the line labelling problem tractable and surjective, ascertaining its outward pointing normal vectors. Whorospheres best to be from someplace else: 1

Cleverness

0. In my asymptotic direction of travel tracking skill increases by the requirement that maps and targets serve as aids for accuracy: the proliferation of genius; a decade of heavy labor, they can rise to the full advertised energy of the machine, compromisers compromised, suitable applicants invited for competititve interview, passing, passing through matter virtually unhindered and difficult to detect. Subtract uniqueness from the multiplicity to be constituted; each target written at *n*-1 dimensions, made not born in this employability of artists overcome by packing hierarchies of information, a dense locale of well-organised systems of connection ignorant that every non-recursive set must be complicated in a very essential way, paper folding and cutting, disrupt backing of stationary manuscripts. The music of nonalgorithmic voices, neither reflexive match between properties of content, properties of the vehicle that carry it is. Given this, there seems to be little motivation for: 1

Colours

0. Grey accepts: Brown. Black changed dirty shirts, Gold, daughters, pierced and bronze. Never underestimate one effect as an attractor, any terminating stream of fixed payments over a specified time while we watch and hope to spray bodily fluids across your belly. Seminal plasma the nutrients from our decomposing synesaethesia. The reminder of what might be missed, what could have been, remarkably paradisiacal only less so now with more fruit, thick and creamy. Living where cooperative insurance was a case in point the pattern of net and skin presupposes Alzheimer's is not refuge from knowing. Of scatology and eschatology, I know now what I didn't know in the beginning. You have been loved. Unspeakable. Epiphenomenal written. Pause please as fish the verb To fledge, the source adds little to our understanding. Interruption working like an Ottoman in a tunnel, interference, strange compact forms – discrete breathers – inspire: 1

Compromise

0. We published. With the venue only adequate – commensurate/concommittant to the dispositive company passed by the demand mapping serves as aids for accurate measurement. Cumulative mistakes in airport or other transport hubs, times, tables, tannoi annoyances crying at details to tidy imagination for reasonableness. Artists as trophies, performance measures the softer option agreed. Demands, reasonable demands couched in repeated reasonableness, boredom conditioning order can create word increments when one axiom or other is relaxed; evaluation of a tuple never fails in any subordinating allowance, bar deliberate martydom right or wrong (crossing the e-picket just once surjectively characterizes language deterioration, indifferent attitude, and appearing first as memory decline, over several years, destroying cognition, personality, ability to function. Confusion & restlessness/you can't remember the end forever until everything, under the irrevocable symmetry lost, is the same except regret: 1

Dialect

0. His lyric cul-de-sac, his corrupt hegemonic variant, his with the meaning is the use; the universe of all small types, which contains names for all the types. Evaluation of a tuple will never fail any subordinate variety any non-standard vocabulary making this thing other: scrawp, ascribe to, ratify, make reasonable: a garden-design mind. Categories with Families are to Categories with Attributes sadly this is harder to read as a second language harmonious with substitution – against his type of well-founded arborescence, who the fuck cares iff she celebrates with bad gratitude but no notable venue. Her usual function space arises as a special case gifted when they do not fear change. So translation symptoms continue as daily torment and will do, bijective to someone non-local: values in each and all, a proposition here identified with its proofs is the same everywhere, that is: matching his and hers. Statues accrue endlessly. You never lose the accent, whereas formulas that are 'true', blanket intuition as iff a proof can be constructed for it. If small changes can produce a broken jump the function is said to be discontinuous: 1

Doubt

0. Is the hesitant man falling or praying? Is it formally sufficient to rely on oscillating marginal words, collating parallel texts against the geometry of times, one note rather than another, wrong numbers, tables, details curled up with cumulative mistakes? Iff disorder will increase as well-organised systems are left to themselves, is politeness partly absolute order over chaos? Pleasant order creating order from disorder cleaves to the choice else it would not be free, thus for those who defended this view the answer to the question "Could courtesy be a fused-group?" Iff both are open, then despite all possibilities to fall, the two possibilities miraculously cancel each other out: the same thought said in another way? So no then. All interpersonal comparisons systematically impossible (along with grey) the scarce theorem of contradiction should die and even if we die first we were better – bullish and triumphant (either way), aspiring to dutchness – always come to: 1

Entscheidungsproblem

0. is there some procedure which could solve all problems one after the other? She killed to see what it would feel like, if any letter or number replaced by itself is identical, when I could have told her that it feels the same or indistinguishable from it. Without the axiom of choice, (belonging to some sculpturally deceived class) the vote, the city the *same* after each material replacement. Ay, marry consistency, to risk fianchetto equiconsistency: most disciplines can be reduced, formalizable within itself; as impossible as say naming the measurement process highest when the transaction finishes – and this happens over an interval one cannot point to. The laws governing the phenomena more complex and margins who share this general repugnance, aspiring regardless, transgress reproduction of the relations of production pulling our ladder up to test behind us. The definition of permission; the immemorial question with no allegorical significance for some classes – one alternative over another – could be "determining" the choice, else it would not be free thus for each: 1

Epigones

0. Second-rate or loosely prehensile, our heroes forgotten, the principle of least privilege delegated accrues for sun kings, sons richly apprenticed His, corrupt variance toward the meaning in its use; the universe of all small types, which contains names for all the attributes forgotten; facilitating removal of exotics as nonalgorithmic monuments: telomeres thin between every regeneration. Children haunt with the smell of butchery, cost and elections deplete memory of us, heroes, our movements recorded and forgotten, from one traffic light junction to the next top of the range sports car accelerates ostentatiously away to wait to surge by system of apologia-inertia by proxy's excluded other, middle and below, effectiveness derogating to 'the same point in space repeated times' as last season's telomeres thinned toward brown, became fashionably black, decisionally incapacitated by golden lineage, modelled proudly by Akhenaten's daughters, with tanned, luxuriant, pierced bellies, the statute delegation: we were all epigones will be again, singular in the infernal drilling noise of extractor fans. A changed voice would stand out saying: one day you will be someone who lived long ago: 1

Eugenics

0. a phenomenon (1984) described weeds such as people alteration of the species for sociological purposes (bruised in old sores to cleanse dry) criminal degenerates and race facilitating removal of exotics (faith in other motivation – well-organised systems of voluntary unconscious selection friendly to natural impact of invasives in relation to direct competition (in every county of this dysgenic land (killed to confirm field identifications) most successful introduced invaders (tough phlegm and clammy humours (to open obstructions of liver and spleen)) to protect the united states (against "indiscriminate immigration (ill or undernourished or (using a decoction of two) whether artwork or not must comply with those laws (withal 'beneficence' leans heavily towards utility (without killing the specimen some type specimen) "won't accept the idea they are in general second rate we) (would be a more fateful step than any previously) the 'what it's like' character of mental states, bifurcated into hard to reach groups, mutually nonadjacent and unnatural selection: unbeknownst: 1

Expectation

0. what it is for the "given" to be "taken"; Who I was What was I When was it Where was I an event whose probability is not 0. The absolute future may not be well-defined for every inability to develop its own knowledge-intensive growth has not had immediate negative effects on aggregate measures of prosperity. Or as fools once said: building a new formation for common space omitting the fundamental importance of ISBN. 0: doesn't bode well and compromised truth measures the lower threshold described as 'no more than one at or below.' The absolute future of the event consists of all events which can be causally affected by Who the fuck cares is putting it too strongly in an equilibria reducing complexities. *Note* no upper threshold definition – normality must always be paid for, with quiescence, stupidity, criminality, inertia, certainty. To accept barbarous dissolution, inevitably the worst thing that happened was the passing of the short Age of the Counter Tenor. Struggle against torpor, the evanescence and disappearance of that which seems worthwhile to be pursued, tracked, gathered, against a choice of mildnesses:
1

Faces

0. Since the invention of colour portraiture men never swim unless they can; this area lights up in response. Motionless, observed of all observers, eye contact eyes innocent, seen not only if the waiter had looked up just then my guilty slot repetition, my allocated table, prepersonal intensity corresponding to the passage from one experiential state of the expression to another implying an augmentation or diminution in that body's capacity to act. The embarrassment directed and turned from. He suggested that I be programmed – a relation between situations allows yourself to say how close each one compatible with local actions is or the same expression and closest response to the starting situation plus an extra micro-tactical ingredient. The hungry asymmetrical gaze prevents medicine from draining down the tear duct, preparation that old couples could only cleave together until they are cleaved apart in forgetful refuge windows for learning recognition as cumulative mistakes, from skull sinuses, continuously draining fluid turning into something hard, nut-like, slow liver quick, a pathogen of space: 1

Family

0. Rituals built the next level of reality; family rituals colourless not like sleep which has detained flickering but like being dead – nothing, nothing to eat. Thinning between every generation translated into my encopresis drill and cleaving together attributes and, in their turn, vicariant children haunting with the smell of butchery disinterested finality – if they escape into the world for human development a more profound attachment to non-living things. Heart-warming bond breaking requires energy measured by *how many fluents change:* "You can't remember the start", where 'distance' means 'days go by'. Is it responsible to break the hierarchy of mediations or self-preservation? Renormalisation avoids those infinities, but vagueness thins a trapped null surface; so the absolute future may not be well-defined for every event, nativity sleep-walked away from (for example killing your grandmother, preventing your birth is commonly cited) annoying as dada, backward referral of unconscious information avoids the causal, the paradox, decoherence, dreams and rescue from the unfortunate role of illusory epiphenomenon: 1

First

0. afternoon sunshine enlightened adornment turns after so many centuries, the total light process after denunciation of the reason for rebelling, separate shameless and fearless, the irreflexive observed of all observers made relevant no more than one at or below lower individual thresholds, truth measures originality, disgraced out of context, shout look down. When it stopped growing started breaking down the position to be below for this indicator becomes thin ice pointed out as the universal spread of dangerous skating. Brown. Black. Gold. Mere functionaries, epigones and celebrated progeny respect only themselves again. By no means complete; nor are they safe in extreme abuse creativity replacing both the pause of autumn, the way low sunlight falls on red berries and the melancholy pleasure of remembering lost. The tone of lenient council can return after their revolt from protection; a hand holding out graces, favours, and immunities. The delusive plausibilities equals who is the child star's famous father?: 1

Fishing

0. The most impactful explanatory ignorance, the absence of loss; generally regarded as bad taste, folding, by proxy, rewarded for nothing in homage to a crude rather than vicious origin. Let's not pass it down it is not deserved: callow relentless epigones, one once during our lifetime and once to die within a week of its languorous spawning. The nutrients from our decomposing bodies help distract their mock anxious totality of living, waiting insofar as one belongs to it. They undergo physiological changes that allow them to adapt to colonizing new areas, replenishing weak populations, reflux as verb for human development more profoundly attached to non-living things. Like all men, scared of big leaves, endurance pain, the old become attractive like a future with our past, a future entertainingly bleak for vertebrates. They get food, they create litter, they mature. Particular factors for population's health: youth doesn't get killed or eaten, incubating mediated identities returning in one to two weeks as long as she is able before anticipated and unrealised dying moments of beauty replaced with concepts of soapy attraction: 1

Fluents

0. no two prosopagnosics are the same but this may still be desirable. Discrete breathers parametrise pseudogenes carrying the (de)merits of varieties of destructive encopresis drill the orthodox treatment of the frame problem of actions (labelled transitions between situation descriptions) he may be the only thing happening there, him, (or her) useful work output divided by the energy having parallels in psychopathy checklist scoring. Give yourself relations between situations which allow you to say how *close* they are to each other and otherwise are closest to the starting situation plus an extra ingredient – we can ignore the risk register jargon current; base category negations true in that state decomposed into divided parts containing the action and the fluents relevant to that action, but we probably don't want products from the vocabulary so badly weakened. Think draw posets in absolute futures that can juxtapose be surpassed by: 1

Hesitation

0. Standing non-monotonic alongside each other weighing solitude is a project. Management weakness many forms of probabilistic reasoning fail to satisfy Cut. To see in time we have the solidity of buildings in this space or underground symbolism. (In fact, it can shrink) Every day in which grey reasoners draw conclusions tentatively, pretending to put forward a project of universal citizenship because of the sex of conclusions. Eschatology warranted on the basis of a given knowledge base does not increase with the size of the knowledge base itself reserving the right to retract them, I so want this to end. Tossing a coin always provided the right answer. Toward this end intensifying the pervasiveness of its intervention over every element of the harsh abundance. The length of the proof does not affect the degree to which the assumptions support lotteries or magic thinking; the ultimate power of your knife can be put aside, hood removed and let her go, leaving sleep to society as police are to dreams: 1

Houses

0. Vitruvian in determinedly outside. Of somewhere else, empty rooms, once empty, somewhere someone else, something somewhere someone else. Madeiraised. Nuclear unit composition in a hidden place of imbalance and ill-considered, Cartesian headphony coffin lining family rituals, colourless not like sleep. Euripides women carrying the news of loss. Vicariance perversely rotating, inheriting weak model fragments I couldn't care less, room vocabulary of windows of geometry generated in machines designed for the purpose more fullerene than their products. Renormalisation within building regulation would in this case would be a fine object, a still life. Changing light: 1

Interference

0. Is this the best that can be hoped for? we-are-o-so-dangerous the new manifesto, celebrating ineffectiveness in diagram horizons more than or equal to the first range of hills that encircles the scanty vale of human life: really the apparent horizon a surface defined as the boundary between light rays which are directed outwards and moving outwards, and those directed outwards but moving inwards. My far-field diffraction denies allegiance now and less more then. Fantasy desert and steppe poets, game-level resistance, reinforce the torsion insistent constriction blanketing a globe at a scale of one to one. Immediate nonadjacency is also the interference pattern forward, auxetic discrete breathers travelling only with gestures of European (or other) smatterings and chess dialects. Tmesis therefore we are. Rejecting nature in a good way any closeness suitable to divergent boundaries ends in hospital passing with past teleology: 1

Islam

0. so says algorithm: to transform every number into 19 Compendious Book on Calculation by Completion enshrines all around anthropic argument verb sensitive to assumption completes operation moving a negative quantity from one side of the equation to the other side with changing its commutation all the same. These so irretrievable, the overstaid fraction, unicyclic taste These so irretrievable, the overstaid fraction, auxetic ideas report adverse events and deterred from becoming expert witnesses exact to every single letter the system the system the system. A cloud appeared and enveloped them, a voice came from the cloud, a physical transportation, nor loud-voiced in streets no human conjecture is involved, proving its own consistency to be a basic telomere assumption, on number theory, on statistics analogy admonition against misinterpretation, restoration and compensation. Taste the touch validity with respect to substructures; apostasy the pun of impenetrability according to looking at this girl. The underachiever anomaly applies even with the name change where it is the last word on page: 1

Lassitude

0. Sleeps a moment fallen on snowy steps. Will resignation to decay happily (few can resist). Martyrdom can only be given not taken, invited through the rejection of pension arrangements, to tire of the age spent and starving – on the street can still be screaming at the storm – despite compulsory annuity solutions. Regardless, they never allow shock in production & consumption, nothing collapses. Proceeding by exhaustion, from this great mass of details decomposed into a small part containing action, relinquishing cognition, personality, rather than fearing disability to function, embracing our counter-finality. Reject. Peace doesn't tell us about the fate of fluents not affected by aphasia we can have two different, but equivalent, fears; subversion only as revolt is co-opted if there are simply a finite number of models, these propositional genes are hence vocabulary dependent: bodies in motion or at rest are freed momentarily prior to treatment for concussion: something missing: 1

Lime

0. Queuing. Every aesthetic has a compulsory fire exit. Sufficient safety assessments laid out to leave this frame reminder of corridors the meniscus of habit, a vestige normalcy, a past act, that theorem about outside time to die voiceless voting for the oath of loyalty. Green newly black to get off a stationary maceration, angular rotation about that axis unrefreshed. Reading newspapers, listening to radio, download charts, the public and a fixed description is not sensitive to a starting time we have constant lowered energy. Slaked our worldlines tight circle to orbital consolations, His presidential manner their enthusiasm to cause slow dissolve, praise be upon him. These so irretrievable ugly signs pointing only to concrete utility and back alleys: 1

Lottery

0. Standing alongside each other, we fluents only appear to act, as a practico-inert whole stochastic thickness towards interchangeability and the instrumental inspires every individual to solitary behaviours – random solitude as a project. Lying awake at night the totality of living humans, as one belongs to it, imagines a continuum between nothing, indolence, ultraparallel industry and employment of friends and artist trophies. Touching this or that invoking indeterminate causalities: in time we have assurance solidity of [centre] buildings in this space. Regeneration of small empty ghost towns with no raison d'etre. Failure to predict. Not having had the experience; to organise oneself in front, to chair the panel. Any exceptions too indeterminate laws of decency overwhelm oscillation's agitated senses, a conic god-aesthetic penis as a good luck charm at the front door thus protected: magic thinking: alarmed by the corrupting influence; alarmed by corrupting influence: the ratio of desperation to losing hope: 1

Method

0. Iff means testing is a system of inertia by proxy of that excluded middle. Iff they would sell the people's park, pulling the ladder up to test behind us. (Obsequious masses arise) iff law asserts an equivalent negation, aspiring to dutchness, (practical and living) one should never cross an e-picket. Rebelling and revolting, no more deluded by reaction, able to deny, subtracting a firming aspect from the law, demanding a definite life construct "Icouldhaveenjoyedsocialism"; retrodicted darkness generated inexorable artificial rules, authors find hope in their framework of grace and means, aspiring to overview all the texts submitted and accumulate authority to help run their Inquisition. (To sacrifice us to their pride) iff dreams be responsible, external drivers affect workforce planning, segmentation into minutes, morning consequence of industrial discipline; where each tyranny fixes his sign. Iff a passage leads to the author where he began: (the People's Flag) alone with his own text, categorically ignorant the text must seek selflessly immemorial after us, but stand within Her sweeping redness: 1

Moment

0. of turning when mythically heroes arrive at the same time at the same place. And treatise on the way to induce angular rotation of an object to spin faster. Bond breaking requires energy, so can absence give an example of when you have made a mistake and what lessons solidify through non-zero into a rational number happening. The concentrated axis (we happy few asymptotically combine to form a fused-group) – self reflexive, distainful of the larger wheel that takes more effort to accelerate, moments of inertia moving/shifting interference; time appointed explosive only for observers who are 'stationary' preserving all distances. Now. How long does a moment require? The teleology of shamans, soloists and messiahs, the coming together of serial nonalgorithmic certainty and stochastic heroes' sensory inputs up to 500 milliseconds for the design and construction of bridges, the observers referral of unconscious information avoids the tickbox, the paradox, decoherence, dreams and decay from the compromising role of distracting epiphenomenonal justifications: meanwhile/moreover we are the ones: 1

Neither

0. the slender margin, an opera, nor an anti-opera tainted by love, the connotation of pairwise disjoint whether artwork or not must comply with those laws either one cannot pre-empt and material adequacy, service resilient populations with which few can disagree appears to be the same thought said, the moment of decoherence repeated in another way – a meditation on self-awareness coloured by pungent ahistoricism; unsettling sonorities webbed on the other, singularities that serve to rupture and renew normative discourse always emerge from interstices. Abelian at its atonal margin and most liberating. Reading can hear it calling me the way it used to be; quiet activist renormalisation makes special default Monotony to spatial disorientation. To disagree arises as a special case gifted when the range does not fear change, a tuple of complex numbers accepted as if small changes can produce a broken jump, the revelation of discrete breathers. Iff the import of monotony is that: 1

Number

0. every individual would be found to be perfectly distinguishable from others: with armchair rapists wishing it could be their hierarchy of mediations: sequences of keys in locks the same in every house permits sequential arbitrary choices. Lost to automated beauty stupidity of highways and government anthrometrics. Iff asked, each is the same as the Others to the extent that he is himself, lovers, friends, customers, whores, commodity strangers, girls on the beach, dreams, jobs, locations, houses – maybe instances of familiarity: subtracting that firming aspect relative of normal controls in the hope some day in the colonized sector you will be one of those who lived long ago. The End. Of Greatness some infinities are bigger than others and this plurality of separations just like being in organized war integration of individuals into negative separate groups. That grey area we can all feel passionate about. All information about anatomy could be reduced to a set of identifications which could be system with plotters and the plotted streets that precede this: 1

Objects

0. Speaking of the thing has spoken to compose momentum states out of position states, to represent things as they are worked-on matter decomposition matters the same kind of solidity as your table, your chair; fixated on things in evacuation, for human development the more profound attachment to non-living things. An internet of things. A loss of human presence will eliminate any imaginary components, discrete breathers, reified, moment thickness, so be in two qualities at once – typically the right hand controls the pitch and the left controls volume real valued experiment outcomes. Touch the true use of measurement only for presence. There are some technical caveats as to what requirements the formal statement representing the screaming banality of detail, drop, fall, ignore. Face gravity bleeding through reassurance, the weak force where headaches gust from. Syndromes of irritability, of scarce items, things you can't have things that stop for noreason, details extreme, its refusal to acknowledge. I embrace and curse you in the last commutation: 1

Palindrome

0. public pitch deafness; to aspire to the condition of Goya, and you wonder what this horror is doing to your long term health, in a chromatic scale the notion of backward progress, and any “dare to know” or “dare to be wise”, (overleaf) bit by bit reinforced concrete foundations, street grids for entertainment and retail more than one consecutive semitone sense that all experience is future-directed with the specific, overwriting individual letters with the same, calculated cheaper epigones to supersede texture timbre and dynamics as primary of gestures. Fuck such as flagstone paving and road building and licenses to gather and the requirement for public liability insurance, more than cobbles which could be thrown, superplasticisers or thinners with properties analogous to those of subscript, the underwritten overwritten, (sound without definite pitch, an even distribution of all frequencies): 1

Place

0. matching his and hers museums like city, taxonomically organized knowledge, we presuppose subclasses inherit properties from superclasses: city equiconsistent with cities, parallel except to collaborate with a suitable non-venue. The holy trinity of any three vegetables in local cuisine, if any letter or number replaced by itself is identical, street plans are either radial or linear or some homotopic interference pattern over bomb sockets or ordinariness, located at the far end of a tree of blood vessels. The place and the placing matter little and for clarity, for order, for visa, the language. Failure to predict is unrelated to having the categories of repetition, geography and external sensations of breeze, sunlight and traffic, to pre-empt a future self. You go there, all things are made. Foundations exposed under glass and viewing microtones of breath between the negative integration of individuals into separate groups, in aisles in anonymous street pleasure thinking (") this is a new: 1

Poem

0. Speaking of Text Has Spoken of the hottest day, ice cold cider competing with the sun, the heat and cold of bodily effects; Suppose a thing is sitting on the edge of a table, how did it not go backwards from the floor to a still-life, an old clock ticking, opening the controlled shipment (language) adds a fresh embarrassment, fresh flowers appointed explosive to a moving/shifting interference containing enough resources to describe that situation. His lyric cul-de-sac, friendly to nature, bucolic idylls devoutly promoted over other plant species must be effected. Condensation decoheres a droplet about to slip down. Boolean, the text past pain replaces memory, pseudogenic decomposed into modules, decomposition matters to text's comprehensibility and maintainability. Light appears blue, the sky appears immediate knowledge backed by axiom of choice and its object, effective coupling, measures how much extra perturbation, a given perturbation generates, awards, dialects, compromises, obsequies sung or silent: 1

Pornography

0. The six types, with modern notations, are: squares equal roots; squares equal number; roots equal number; squares and roots equal number; squares and number equal roots; roots and number equal squares. Solipsism and autism. Temples and churches. Started at a young age. Cars return to city safety passed first outskirt Hindus, mosques, Witnesses' Halls. View practico-inert slideshows; prognosis varies from hope here to fear there, fear here to hope touched with oil. A simile of divergent boundaries, in their mirrors who is the difference between the whore and the hairdresser? Together with scholars who could read and understand them, but Vitruvian children stalk with charges of religious defamation tastier than a plateful of every number looks like nineteen to those looking for lubricious accident – as you are – unreasonable an open austere conservative to abstract expressionism promoted under the tourism's guise to compose everything in terms of the human body and its perfect proportions. The rest is meat ornament. The name chosen at random: 1

Professionalism

0. The property of 'stemness' is elusive and other static and abstract forms – the real business end of the tumour but we cannot demonstrate both simultaneously his interpretation is the interpretation. A pre-established harmony. A hierarchy of mediations. Bullet points intensifying the effectiveness of its intervention over surpassable possibilities and narratives of substantive public purpose. The everyday over the quotidian. A paradigm shift fuck knows how the illustration relates compromise to the muddy flow from dark colours and texts to concentrations of gold within the house of Akhenaten. A listener with no experience of colour is neither democratic nor rhetorical convention embodied in court idiocy demerits balance despite the smell of tobacco and sickness, the autograph of threat assessment demands our right to vote for flatness, the continuous draining of fluids, flimsy epigones undetected in a host during the latency period, which won't touch them personally endangering the species as a whole. For their own good. Separation supported by necessary caring services: what triggers memory: 1

Quiescence

0. Scuttering under a blue cloth within the inquorate grain of memory, can rigidity be said? As hero as shaman. Quotidian fantasy too direct competition for resources, travelling that demands special kinds of travel insurance. Fluents have no time to relax and straighten before celebrated release in flexural waves. Its shattering energy. A lantern to find an honest man? Some particles escape through evaporation, also that microwater bacterially small in the matrix of solidity. We must accept. Direction of travel statements imposed bijective quietus, spending patterns, election to representative bodies more serial measured in responsibility quorum. Monument lions drowned out formants immobilised in narrow happy-clappy tunes. La, la, la for the rest complete transfusions ensure none of the recipient's blood is left at the scene; though surgeon's forgotten instruments as a verb for human development starred ill I aspire as a critical advice giver: the world looms the same everywhere: 1

Reassurance

0. Wherein this stone hasn't cracked there I have a life someone braver lives. Between pendant vertex placed we. Forget tyranny – it is too late for them because dances in light cones happened through those places and pleasures – irreflexive of orthopaedic distortion, hearing loss, spectacles even, to magnify to the classical level) both position and momentum accurate at the same time Reward Points savoured the gutter localised in space, but there is a certain spread; limewise we can never lay claim to the amplitude probability. Plenitude moments with no space in between objects every moment thickened though idiocy surrounds and suffocates, faces will not be necessary to hum; maybe not as good as this one but every word counts, a gag relieves embarrassment during whipping he doesn't weep for what he has lost but for the running out of time in which to make each one happy. Happy – a slender margin more and less. What if the leakage is coming the other way? So I deny allegiance in advance of anything can happen does happen: 1

Reciprocity

0. Among equals every friendship asymptote leans heavily towards *any* closeness order we like tenderness by suitable choice of vocabulary: fused groups collected together as stable alloys, our description not sensitive to a starting time will have constant energy. You do find people have phenomenal capacity, deeply intersecting an infinite number of times. Less serial, this small fusion supporting even when they lose – limbic symmetry of everyone's relations to each other, neither one contains the other. Abelian and free. Performed formants thus permitting longer musical notes to be sustained often over huge distances and times, the more precise the delight we feel in its frequency. Individuals touching intimately feel its vibrations, celebrate the humour of unexpected beats, art and exchange conducive to simply connected space, two points can be continuously transformed into every other, conformally and bijectively mapped emotions good despite rules that the proposition adds nothing: 1

Sculpture

0. The object of making your opponent weep descriptions between the upper and lower structures in vertebrates forming the framework of the mouth, containing the teeth, the parts of tool or machine. That body language material with the tongue intropunitive instead of angry, anger our faults are most obvious as nothing hides them breasts move as sacks of liquid dynamic contents. The knife fixation on things in evaluation, of sweat-scented straps forward and back in the infantile world of ready-made values, woman, the happy or resigned slave lives allowing both misogyny and visionary context. Scattering amplitude internationally is that difference in any given place. Choice language to present material realities, histories that I only deal with divergent objects and all translatable to stand outside a less human presence more profound for their human attachment to non-living things and construction of bridges to be crossed as opposed too catalogued: 1

Shaman

0. the proliferation of genius, both sides of detection, psychopathy checklist high scores competititive interview procedure: the more accurately the position is measured, the less accurately the momentum is determined passing through matter virtually unhindered, moreover, difficult to detect turning that fleshy muscular organ. Nonalgorithmic celebrated freedom from constraint, stem cells disguised faith can experiences contradict this optimistic determinism without the confusion of categories. Resurrect the idea action's fabric synonymous with its content. Facticity without 2Mùan 1bpö/ no reality being in more than one place at one time. Confidence in extrapolating and it was called the singularity, antonymous to modern systemic sensory inputs bridged with engineering software, public sector financial incompetence, flattened out epiphenomenal justifications – sighs, epiphanous sighs; for the irreflexive how the autumn sunlight patterns dust over wood grain intersected with baritone shadows: 1

Singularity

0. *Every absolute beginning requires the absolute solitude* individually of the reformer or founder individually firewalled with headphones, ligeti in public, only non-zero within ourselves, the amount of each does not depend on the presence of the other, passing vicariant streets, conserved so long as the masses did not interact; confined plurality of solitudes: we all muffled these people are not concerned, or for one another – Eased forgetting melody and comfort of signs repeating back reassurances, pastoral wistfulness despite trenchantly concreted contexts. Cities delight, surjective experience, microtones of breath, walking soundtrack sharper – though we never dance in the streets – presenting a tinny aspect inspires individuals/particles to solitary behaviour. Gates, boarding, not boarding, no one sits next to me, windows blacked out, revving at the lights to accelerate to the lights minus the big connection. Some infinities are bigger than others and this dizzying plurality separates groups, the negative integration of individuals into separate groups, in aisles in anonymous streets pleasure: 1

Tmesis

0. I the (xenodiverse) first (macrofouled) shall (fear) be (choking) last areas of divergent boundary (singularities that abound to rupture) lime (rapacious parenthesis) otherwise lawful activity (it) spreads at the bottom of the viscous puddle, at the bottom of (time) under (see below) Natural beauty (it) is a small happiness of Nausea: Nausea is not inside me "measures" for (its) protection of (danger) – *so:* ignore the gaps between cities is the best (the (so-called) "Habitats Directive) policy plants prohibits (unauthorised) intentional uprooting (nature's cleansing) species – restless – restless – restless picking, uprooting or inherited into everything (decaying) pieces of carpet, rotting (from maladaptive) shoes and abundance of non biodegradable items particularly shiny vinyl records (or) (seemingly) incidental (*Shisho*) actions as unavoidable results of steganography (abhors ellipsis): obvious (undersocialized) work strives for authenticity: 1

Translation

0. The crisis in translation is bollocks – with no allegorical significance – one alternative over algebraic notation – sadly chess is harder to read as a second language. So translation symptoms continue as a daily torment and will do, bijective to someone non-local: a proposition identified with the type of its proofs here is the same everywhere, that is: types which contain values, aspiring to dutchness, the extension of the abnormality predicate should be minimal words, books back to east front to west front or back books interchangeable depending on east or west orientation. Fervently the postal analogy to understand the compositional advantages of asymmetric system, internets of things, where language died located at the far end of a tree of blood vessels, leaving only his lyric cul-de-sac, dialects, and foundations exposed under glass, microtones of fucking, negative, integration of individuals into separate groups hope for specific objects and they are all translatable into another language, values in each and:

1

Underachievement

0. Verbs could do and *could* do. The underachiever anomaly why duration or amount or distribution form fault for failing. Invitation to the norm. Pi replaced by PIN. Some measure of goodness's formal invitation. Naming evil is simply naming that which is contraindicated, so twenty numbers define everything except regret; there is no such number of likewise no such world past pain reasonableness, but time allocation (dying young) is a poor excuse. Nothing too, its factual content and fear of loss is not connected to the divine attacks. Like the figurative consensus with no significance – for some nepotism – occupying the same space at the same time, in this telomere insurance the thin fibre of a situation should contain enough resources to describe only that situation. Mutually nonadjacent: unbeknownst, rigour it demands: as if prior deliberations chain explanation to certain early formative stages this route hard to sustain in token events and other distances the simplest poset add: 1

Vinculum

0. "interrupted pendulum" with equal probability finding grains spinning up or down, some part which cannot be assessed, only non-zero within ourselves, and the amount of each does not depend on the presence of the other: fundamentally non-local fields are to accelerations as falling is to shopping, tales of passing vicariance, conserved so long as the masses did not interact; preyed on and preying, fearful of collision preyed on and preying between. Prognosis varies from hope here to fear there and fear here and hope there. Senescent memory loss, language deterioration, poor judgment appearing first as function. Under the continuous symmetry of time translation symptoms continue as a daily torment and despite all our bijective vinculum to someone non-local; conjugate variables appear separated, that old couple can only cleave together until they are cleaved apart, the system of fear to curl up with eschatology, a smell like tobacco, tired leather and urine and loss: you can't remember the end all the time. So ending matters only in its manner, it's only martyrdom iff lives are ultraparallel: 1

Whorosphere

0. O and there's literature don't forget(.) it all depends. Reciprocal shaken negation of the barefoot. Masturbation backslash scientific method a framework of grace/means kissed the girls and made them cry; when the boys came out to play so religion rarely offers: Progress must be careful what we pretend to be – winning can be similar to dying: disoriented men and aborted a little conception at its birth. Watch where you're walking counting the cracks, the sudden realization that even embracing them does not make you safe. The young regimented in tonality hear it as white noise, shiny aspirants to the lifestyle of Akhenaten's daughters; Just Me; vitreous humour breasts dynamic in cold choice toss of the coin while we watch hope to spray, meat smells warmth unable to discern. Embodied exo- and endogenetic processes are brought into close proximity here, my theory, with no actual coupling parameters, of scatology and eschatology, of unfashionable learning and lewdness, ardent as octopus, unregulated eroticism of legs in dark streets, drunk from music after monotonous compulsory mountains watching with the lassitude of a (wo)man waiting for matter and meaning seem to be our position – that's over too: 1

Widerstand

0. Commutative Transgression. Complaint over revolt. Revolt over game-level resistance, time. If one of the two routes is open, then that route can be travelled; if the other route is open, then that route can be travelled: iff both are open, then two possibilities miraculously cancel each other out: neither route appears to free. Internal exile limits reasonable compromise to sulking or accept barbarous dissolution, endless war denoting 'reorganization of the urban syntax by means of a series of micro-tactical actions', a musicality if you slipped through the door without saying goodbye or say nothing at the meeting. Expectations. Invalidations: a refugee's working relationship to the distance bound, being, beginning, starting from nothing; to an absolute indispensably necessary state reflective of objective oppositi-judgements. To stand outside in the dispositive geometry of contradiction: starred ill and well, we reject therefore we are: 1

Yggdrasill

0. Twilight and narrow, fiddler's ferry cooling towers, ice cold transference competing with the heat of bodily effects – framed for southerners – gigantic concrete trunks steam foliage, fidelity of shape as motion of the basilar membrane bends stereocilia on the land; language adds fresh embarrassment, fresh flowers teaming in turn excite the associated fibers. A soundscape at its atonal bleakest, nature without the visitor numbers and most liberating aleatory not merely pseudo-randomised algorithms but appearances which manifest neither interior nor exterior; all things being equal, revel if you must in noncomputational spatial disorientation; homotopy between the two bold paths with its colours (sometimes televised nevertheless) scent outskirts the pale as parks are to decoration: local neighbourhoods do not have self-intersections. Storage is revealed or not revealed and so ignore the labile gaps between cities, sensible advice, in thrombosis precaution walking the sleeping aisles with the quaint outdated notions of windy steppe and desert unequal to the libretto from forty thousand feet: 1

Apology

0. pollarded. Inert with targets. Told and giving up within the week is the easy Victorian option now; generally orchestra is diminished by the demand for youthful understanding – a case fatality ratio. Ragnarök partial orders merely travel change, the most successful vertebrates that ever lived. Time for irreflexivity: iff I can be the collapsing material straight away rotations are not commutative. Drippling to the end weakly, you don't want to think any more. Hadja wished, it can't be hermetically sealed: false to worldly, false but this equiconsistent with heroism, without being able to prove it(,) can always be commuted to no(,) waiting for the: 1